Building Spelling Skills GRADE 2

What's in This Book?

Scope and Sequence	2
Teaching the Weekly Unit	4
Spelling Strategies	6
How to Study Your List	7
Sentences for Dictation	8
Take-Home Spelling Lists	10
Weeks 1–30 Activity Pages	20
Forms	
Spelling Record Sheet (class)	140
My Spelling Record (student)	141
End-of-Week Spelling Test Form	142
Blank Spelling List Form	143
Crossword Puzzle Template	144
Parent Letter for Take-Home Lists	145
Student Spelling Dictionaries	146
You Are a Super Speller! Certificate	148
Master Word List (alphabetical)	149
Answer Key	151

Writing: Jo Ellen Moore
Content Editing: Leslie Sorg
Copy Editing: Cathy Harber
Art Direction: Cheryl Puckett
Cover Design: Cheryl Puckett
Illustration: Jim Palmer
Design/Production: Jia-Fang Eubanks
Yuki Meyer

EMC 2706

Evan-Moor.
Helping Children Learn

Visit
teaching-standards.com
to view a correlation
of this book.
This is a free service.

Correlated to Current Standards

Scope and Sequence

Week	Focus	
1	Spell short vowel words	20
2	Spell short vowel words	24
3	Spell short **i** and **a** short words; Spell words in the -**all** and -**and** families	28
4	Spell short vowel words; Spell words with **or**; Recognize homophones **four** and **for**; Recognize the words **I** and **we**	32
5	Review short vowel words; Spell long vowel words with silent **e**	36
6	Spell words with the long **e** sound spelled **e** or **ee**; Spell short **o** words	40
7	Spell long **o** and long **a** words; Recognize the vowel sound in **do**; Spell words in the -**ind** family; Add the ending -**ing** with no change to the base word	44
8	Review long and short vowel words; Spell words with the consonant digraph **th**; Recognize the short **u** sound in **was** and **of**; Recognize the vowel sound in **a**	48
9	Review short **u**, long **u**, and long **o** words; Recognize the short **u** sound in **some** and **come**; Add the ending -**ing** after doubling the final consonant	52
10	Review long **a** and long **i** words; Spell the vowel sounds in **help**, **here**, and **want**; Add the ending -**ing** after dropping the silent **e**; Recognize homophones	56
11	Spell words with the final consonant blends **nd** and **st**; Spell words with the final consonant digraph **th**; Spell words with the /**k**/ sound spelled **ck**	60
12	Spell words with the long **i** or long **e** sound spelled **y**; Review short and long vowel spelling patterns; Study contractions	64
13	Practice spelling words with double consonants; Distinguish between one- and two-syllable words	68
14	Spell words in the -**oat**, -**ong**, and -**all** families; Spell words with the vowel digraph **aw**	72
15	Spell words with the vowel digraphs **ai** and **ay**; Review long **a** words with silent **e**	76
16	Spell words with the vowel digraph **oo**; Recognize the two sounds of **oo**; Spell words with the initial consonant digraph **wh**	80

Week	Focus
17	Spell words with the vowel digraphs **ow** and **ou**; Recognize the two sounds of **ow** 84
18	Spell words with r-controlled vowels spelled **er**, **ir**, **ur**, and **ar** 88
19	Spell words with initial consonant blends **fl, bl**, and **st**; Spell words in the -**ore**, -**ew**, and -**ing** families 92
20	Spell words ending in **ve**; Spell words with the consonant blends **fr** and **ld**; Spell words with the final consonant digraph **ch**; Recognize the short **u** sound spelled **ove** 96
21	Spell words with the initial /**y**/ sound; Review long **i** words with the silent **e**; Spell words with the initial consonant blend **dr**; Spell words with the vowel digraph **aw** 100
22	Spell words with diphthongs **oi** and **oy**; Spell words that end with -**ther** or -**ter**; Distinguish between one-, two-, and three-syllable words 104
23	Spell words with final consonant digraphs **th** and **sh**; Spell words with final consonant blends **ng** and **nk** 108
24	Review words with the long **i** or long **e** sound spelled **y**; Spell words with the long **e** sound spelled **ea**; Spell words with initial blends **tr** and **fl** 112
25	Spell words with initial consonant blends **tr** and **st**; Add the ending -**ed** after doubling the final consonant; Spell **say** and **said**; Spell words with the short **u** sound 116
26	Spell words with a final **k** or **ck**; Review the two sounds of the vowel digraph **oo** 120
27	Spell words with the blends **pr**, **br**, and **ft**; Spell two-syllable words; Review long **a** words with silent **e**; Spell words with the initial consonant digraph **ch** 124
28	Spell words with the vowel sound in **put** and **could**; Spell words with the diphthongs **ou** and **ow**; Recognize the short **u** sound in **something** 128
29	Review long and short vowel sounds; Listen for the initial consonant digraph **th**; Spell two- and three-syllable words; Recognize homophones (**no**, **know** and **to**, **two**) 132
30	Spell words with initial consonant digraphs **wh** and **th**; Recognize and spell antonyms; Spell compound words; Recognize the short **e** sound in **again** 136

Teaching the Weekly Unit

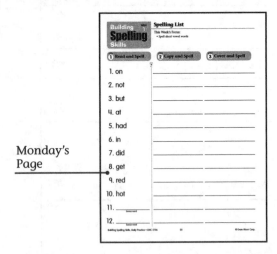

Monday's Page

Strengthening Students' Spelling Skills

Spelling Strategies
Page 6

How to Study Your List
Page 7

At the beginning of the year, reproduce pages 6 and 7 for each student or on an overhead transparency. Review the general steps and strategies, encouraging students to apply them throughout the year.

Monday

Allot ample class time each Monday for introducing the spelling list and having students complete the first page of the unit.

Introducing the Week's Words

Give each student the spelling list for the week. Here are ways to introduce the words:

- Call attention to important consistencies noted in "This Week's Focus," such as a phonetic or structural element. For example, say: *As we read this week's spelling list, notice that all the words have the same vowel sound.*

- Read each word aloud and have students repeat it.

- Provide a model sentence using the word. Have several students give their own sentences.

- If desired, add "bonus words" based on the needs of your class. These may be high-utility words or words that the class is encountering in curricular studies.

Writing the Words

After introducing the words, have students study and write the words on the first page of the unit, following these steps:

Step 1: Read and Spell
Have students read the word and spell it aloud.

Step 2: Copy and Spell
Tell students to copy the word onto the first blank line and spell it again, touching each letter as it is spoken.

Step 3: Cover and Spell
Have students fold the paper along the fold line to cover the spelling words so that only the last column shows. Then have students write the word from memory.

Step 4: Uncover and Check
Tell students to open the paper and check the spelling. Students should touch each letter of the word as they spell it aloud.

Home Connection

Send home a copy of the Parent Letter (page 145) and the Take-Home Spelling List for the week (pages 10–19).

Tuesday   Visual Memory Activities

Have students complete the activities on the second page of the unit. Depending on students' abilities, these activities may be completed as a group or independently.

Wednesday   Word Meaning and Dictation

Have students complete the Word Meaning activity on the third page of the unit. Then use the dictation sentences on pages 8 and 9 to guide students through "My Spelling Dictation." Follow these steps:

1. Ask students to listen to the complete sentence as you read it.

2. Say the sentence in phrases, repeating each phrase one time clearly. Have students repeat the phrase.

3. Wait as students write the phrase.

4. When the whole sentence has been written, read it again, having students touch each word as you say it.

Thursday   Word Study Activities

Have students complete the activities on the fourth page. Depending on students' abilities, these activities may be completed as a group or independently.

Friday   Weekly Test

Friday provides students the chance to take the final test and to retake the dictation they did on Wednesday. A reproducible test form is provided on page 142. After the test, students can record their score on the "My Spelling Record" form (page 141).

Tuesday's Page

Wednesday's Page

Thursday's Page

Friday's Page

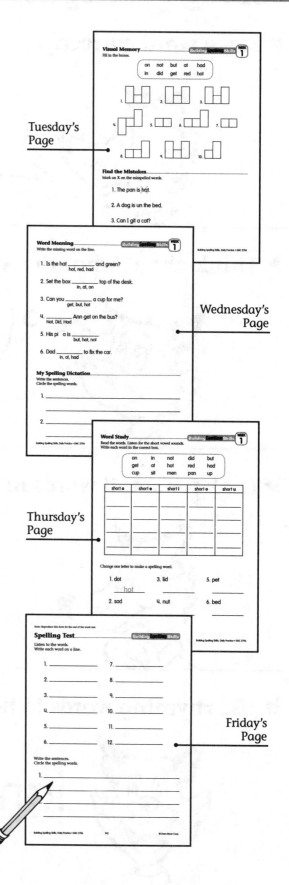

Spelling Strategies

▶ Say a word correctly.

▶ Think about what the word looks like.

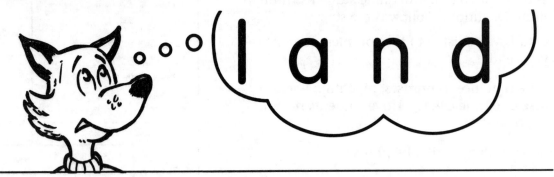

▶ Look for small words in spelling words.

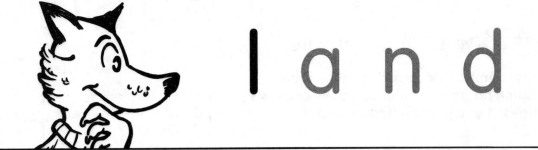

▶ Use rhyming words to help spell a word.

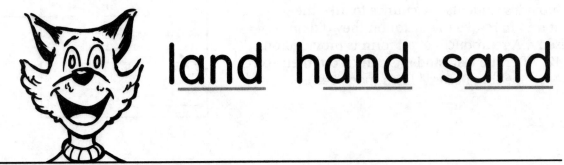

How to Study Your List

❶ Read and Spell

❷ Copy and Spell

❸ Cover and Spell

❹ Uncover and Check

Sentences for Dictation

There are two dictation sentences for each spelling list. Space for sentence dictation is provided on the testing form (see page 142).

- Ask students to listen to the complete sentence as you read it.
- Have students repeat the sentence.
- Read the sentence in phrases, repeating each phrase one time clearly.
- Have students repeat the phrase.
- Allow time for students to write the phrase.
- Read the sentence again, having students touch each word as you say it.

Week	Dictation Sentences
1	Tom **did not get** a **hot** bun. Kim **had on** a **red** hat.
2	His **pet fox** was in a **big box**. Ann **has jam** and an **egg**.
3	**Is his hand small**? Bob **can call his** mom **and** dad.
4	**I** got **it for him**. Can **four men** go **up** in a jet?
5	Lee **came** to **ask** for a **ride**. **Save** a **bone** for the **cute** dog.
6	I **got** to **see** the **queen bee**. Can **he** get **sheep** in the pet **shop**?
7	A **kind** man **gave** us his dog. Am I **going** to **find** the **most** eggs?
8	Max **made that** kite for **them**. **Was the day** hot?
9	**Come** and see the **funny** cat **running home**. **Some** hens **ran** up to **us**.
10	**Help** me get the **two** pigs **into** the pen. I **want to make** a **nice place here to** sit.
11	Tim and Sam **both** ran **fast** at the **end**. She **must pick** the **black** hat.
12	I **liked** the note he **sent** me. The bus **went by my** stop on **time**.
13	**Tell** the **happy little** puppy to sit **still**. **Will** the name come **off** that **letter**?

14   The **fawn** ran **along** the **tall wall**.
Did that **boat belong** to the man in a **long coat**?

15   We had to **wait** for the **rain** to go **away**.
Is he going to **play** games and **paint today**?

16   **Who took** that **good book** to **school**?
He **shook** the box to see **what** was in it.

17   Do not **shout** in **our house**.
Slow down and tell me **about** the **show**.

18   The **girl hurt part** of **her** leg.
Jim and Ann **were** going to **start** the **card** game.

19   A **new ring** at the **store** has a **stone** like a **star**.
Stand still or the bee will **sting** you.

20   Did he **give** the note to his **old friend**?
I **live such** a long way **from** here.

21   Did Mom **yell** when she **saw you draw** on **your dress**?
Drop the ball on that **side** of the **line**.

22   **Father** gave the **other boy** a new **toy**.
My **brother** and **sister** dug in the **soil**.

23   **Thank** you for **this bank** and **these** toys.
Sing a song and **then** make a **wish**.

24   **Why** is the **mean** frog **trying** to get that **fly**?
Will you **read** to me as I **eat** this **treat**?

25   Lee took a **trip** on **train number one**.
Can you **hop** to the **tree** and then **stop**?

26   We **looked** at Pete do a **trick** with a **stick**.
Will the **cook** put the food **back** in his **pack**?

27   The **children** will play a **game** and eat **cake** at the **party**.
Will **people bring gifts** for my **birthday**?

28   Mark **found something brown** under the tree.
Could you help me **pull** my wagon **around** the yard?

29   **Many** children went home **because** it was **very** late.
Did **they** put **anything** in the **water**?

30   Put the box **inside** that car **over there**.
Which dog is running **outside under** the trees?

on

not

but

at

had

in

did

get

red

hot

_____
bonus word

_____
bonus word

as

has

fox

box

mix

egg

jam

pet

nap

big

_____
bonus word

_____
bonus word

his

is

an

and

can

all

call

land

hand

small

_____
bonus word

_____
bonus word

cut

cut

up	add	be
it	ask	see
him	came	got
I	name	she
for	ride	sheep
or	bone	shop
four	save	queen
we	kite	green
man	cute	bee
men	mine	he

_____
bonus word

_____
bonus word

_____
bonus word

_____
bonus word

_____
bonus word

_____
bonus word

cut

cut

no
go
going
most
kind
find
gave
so
do
doing

_____
bonus word

_____
bonus word

the
that
them
day
may
made
was
of
if
a

_____
bonus word

_____
bonus word

some
come
home
fun
funny
run
running
ran
us
use

_____
bonus word

_____
bonus word

cut

cut

place	send	candy
make	pick	went
making	end	sent
help	both	take
here	fast	like
want	last	puppy
nice	must	time
to	just	didn't
two	bath	by
into	black	my

cut

cut

_____
bonus word

_____
bonus word

_____
bonus word

_____
bonus word

_____
bonus word

_____
bonus word

Building Spelling Skills

less
tell
well
will
still
off
letter
little
silly
happy

bonus word

bonus word

Building Spelling Skills

boat
coat
float
long
along
belong
paw
fawn
tall
wall

bonus word

bonus word

Building Spelling Skills

way
away
today
chain
wait
chase
play
played
rain
paint

bonus word

bonus word

cut

cut

too

good

book

shook

school

when

what

took

who

soon

_____
bonus word

_____
bonus word

now

down

how

out

shout

about

our

house

slow

show

_____
bonus word

_____
bonus word

her

girl

turn

hurt

first

were

card

part

start

are

_____
bonus word

_____
bonus word

cut

cut

more	have	you
store	give	your
stand	love	yes
star	from	yell
blew	live	drop
flew	friend	line
new	much	side
stone	such	dress
sting	old	draw
ring	told	saw

_____
bonus word

_____
bonus word

_____
bonus word

_____
bonus word

_____
bonus word

_____
bonus word

cut

cut

boy	this	why
toy	then	try
oil	thing	trying
soil	thank	eat
other	bank	mean
mother	with	read
sister	wish	sunny
boil	think	fly
brother	sing	treat
father	these	each

cut

cut

_____
bonus word

_____
bonus word

_____
bonus word

_____
bonus word

_____
bonus word

_____
bonus word

trip

tree

say

said

hop

train

number

stop

stopped

one

_____
bonus word

_____
bonus word

stick

trick

back

zoo

root

quick

look

looked

pack

cook

_____
bonus word

_____
bonus word

birthday

people

present

candle

cake

children

gift

party

game

bring

_____
bonus word

_____
bonus word

cut

cut

put
push
pull
could
would
found
round
around
something
brown

_____
bonus word

_____
bonus word

they
their
many
any
anything
than
because
know
water
very

_____
bonus word

_____
bonus word

which
where
there
before
after
over
again
inside
outside
under

_____
bonus word

_____
bonus word

cut

cut

Spelling List

This Week's Focus:
- Spell short vowel words

STEP 1 Read and Spell

STEP 2 Copy and Spell

STEP 3 Cover and Spell

fold

1. on

2. not

3. but

4. at

5. had

6. in

7. did

8. get

9. red

10. hot

11. _____
   bonus word

12. _____
   bonus word

Fill in the boxes.

| on | not | but | at | had |
| in | did | get | red | hot |

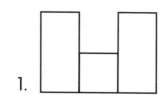
4.

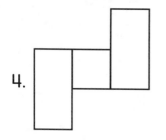
1.

2.

3.

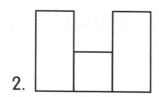
5.

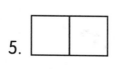

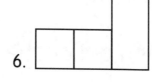
7.

6.

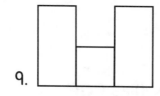
8.

9.

10.

Find the Mistakes

Mark an **X** on the misspelled words.

1. The pan is ~~hat~~.

2. A dog is un the bed.

3. Can I git a cat?

4. His hat is read.

Write the missing word on the line.

1. Is the hat _____ and green?
   hot, red, had

2. Set the box _____ top of the desk.
   in, at, on

3. Can you _____ a cup for me?
   get, but, hot

4. _____ Ann get on the bus?
   Not, Did, Had

5. His pizza is _____.
   but, hot, not

6. Dad _____ to fix the car.
   in, at, had

My Spelling Dictation

Write the sentences.
Circle the spelling words.

1. _____

   _____

2. _____

   _____

Word Study

Read the words. Listen for the short vowel sounds.
Write each word in the correct box.

on	in	not	did	but
get	at	hot	red	had
cup	sit	men	pan	up

short **a**	short **e**	short **i**	short **o**	short **u**
_____	_____	_____	_____	_____
_____	_____	_____	_____	_____
_____	_____	_____	_____	_____
_____	_____	_____	_____	_____

Change one letter to make a spelling word.

1. dot

   _____hot_____

2. sad

   _____

3. lid

   _____

4. nut

   _____

5. pet

   _____

6. bed

   _____

Building Spelling Skills

Spelling List

This Week's Focus:
• Spell short vowel words

STEP 1 Read and Spell

STEP 2 Copy and Spell

STEP 3 Cover and Spell

fold

1. as

2. has

3. fox

4. box

5. mix

6. egg

7. jam

8. pet

9. nap

10. big

11. _____ bonus word

12. _____ bonus word

Fill in the boxes.

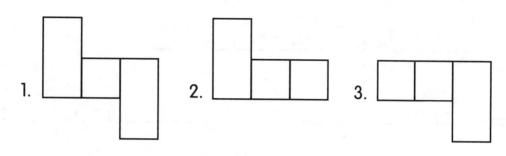

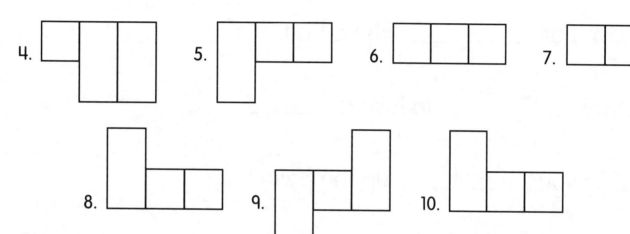

Spell Vowel Sounds

Fill in the missing vowel to make a spelling word. Write **a**, **e**, **i**, **o**, or **u**.

f_o_x   j__m   b__x

__gg   __s   h__s

m__x   n__p   p__t

Fill in the missing words.

as	has	fox	box	mix
egg	jam	pet	nap	big

1. A _____ was in the _____.

2. The hen has a _____ _____ in the nest.

3. Mom ate _____ on a bun.

4. Ned _____ to take a _____.

5. Can you _____ up the paint?

6. Ann has a _____ cat.

My Spelling Dictation

Write the sentences.
Circle the spelling words.

1. _____

_____

2. _____

_____

Word Study

Circle the word in each row that has a different vowel sound.

1. jam   (box)   nap   has

2. pet   egg   mix   red

3. box   as   fox   got

4. it   mix   pet   rip

5. as   nap   big   has

Write the spelling words that rhyme.

as	big	box	egg
nap	jam	mix	pet

1. fox _____   4. pig _____

2. has _____   5. fix _____

3. get _____   6. ham _____

Spelling List

This Week's Focus:
- Spell short **i** and short **a** words
- Spell words in the **-all** and **-and** families

| STEP 1 Read and Spell | STEP 2 Copy and Spell | STEP 3 Cover and Spell |

fold

1. his

2. is

3. an

4. and

5. can

6. all

7. call

8. land

9. hand

10. small

11. _____
    bonus word

12. _____
    bonus word

Fill in the boxes.

his   is   an   and   can
all   call   land   hand   small

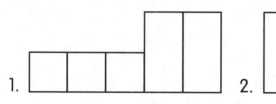
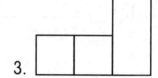
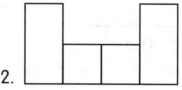

1.   2.   3.

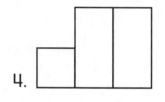

4.   5.   6.   7.

8.   9.   10.

Spell Correctly

Unscramble the letters.

na _____   allsm _____   nac _____

si _____   nad _____   nahd _____

llac _____   shi _____   lal _____

andl _____   lacl _____   ladn _____

Write the missing word on the line.

1. Mom put the cake in a _____ box.
   call, small, ball

2. I cut my _____.
   land, and, hand

3. Did the bug _____ on Kim's leg?
   and, land, hand

4. Pat must _____ his mom.
   small, tall, call

5. Put _____ the pigs in the pen.
   all, small, call

6. Is that _____ ball?
   is, and, his

My Spelling Dictation

Write the sentences.
Circle the spelling words.

1. _____

   _____

2. _____

   _____

Word Study

Add a letter to make a new word.

m an	c an	f an
h en	t en	p en
c oat	b oat	g oat

Write the correct word on each line. Write **four** or **for**.

1. I will get it ___for___ you.

2. The ___four___ men lifted the box.

3. The little hen laid the egg ___for___ you.

4. The goat ate ___four___ bags of corn.

Spelling List

This Week's Focus:
- Review short vowel words
- Spell long vowel words with silent **e**

STEP 1 Read and Spell

STEP 2 Copy and Spell

STEP 3 Cover and Spell

fold

1. add

2. ask

3. came

4. name

5. ride

6. bone

7. save

8. kite

9. cute

10. mine

11. _____
   bonus word

12. _____
   bonus word

Fill in the boxes.

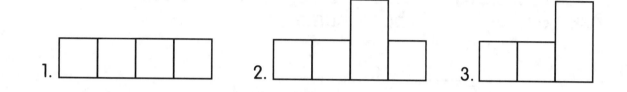

add   ask   came   name   ride
bone   save   kite   cute   mine

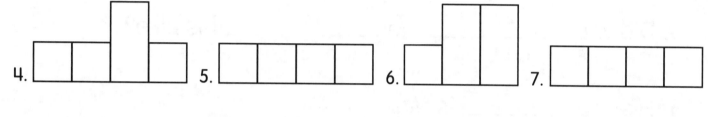

1.

2.

3.

4.

5.

6.

7.

8.

9.

10.

Find the Correct Word

Circle the word that is spelled correctly.

1. kame   came

2. ask   aks

3. kite   kyte

4. ridd   ride

5. qute   cute

6. bone   bown

7. myne   mine

8. add   adde

9. zave   save

10. name   naim

Write the missing words on the lines.

1. The _____ kitten jumped on the bed.
   mine, cute

2. _____ that _____ for the dog.
   Ask, Save   bone, name

3. That red _____ is _____.
   save, kite   mine, add

4. Did you _____ to _____ his bike?
   add, ask   came, ride

5. His _____ is Max.
   came, name

6. Will you _____ these numbers for me?
   add, ride

7. John _____ to the birthday party.
   save, came

My Spelling Dictation

Write the sentences.
Circle the spelling words.

1. _____

   _____

2. _____

   _____

Word Study

Read the words. Listen for the vowel sounds.
Write each word in the correct box.

add	came	ride	up
save	him	men	cute
ask	bone	can	name
got	hand	mine	kite

long vowel sounds	short vowel sounds
_____ _____	_____ _____
_____ _____	_____ _____
_____ _____	_____ _____
_____ _____	_____ _____

Complete each rhyme with a spelling word.

1. Please ask your <u>Dad</u>

   how much to _____.

2. Does this <u>game</u>

   have a _____?

3. I will hold your <u>line</u>

   if you hold _____.

4. The dog is <u>alone</u>

   with his big _____.

Spelling List

This Week's Focus:
- Spell words with the long **e** sound spelled **e** or **ee**
- Spell short **o** words

STEP 1 Read and Spell

STEP 2 Copy and Spell

STEP 3 Cover and Spell

fold

1. be

2. see

3. got

4. she

5. sheep

6. shop

7. queen

8. green

9. bee

10. he

11. _____
   bonus word

12. _____
   bonus word

Visual Memory

Fill in the boxes.

be   see   he   she   sheep

bee   shop   queen   green   got

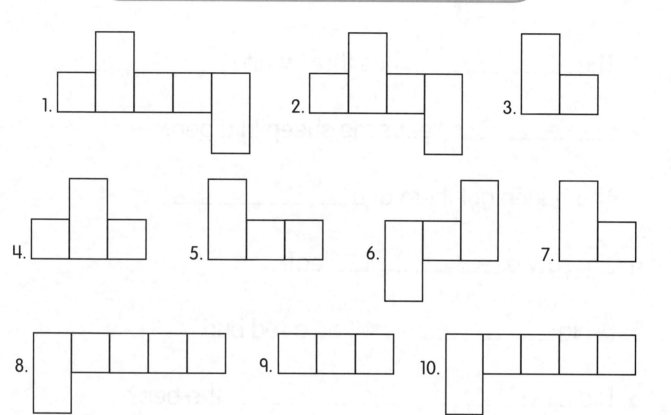

Spell Vowel Sounds

What is missing? Write **e** or **ee**.

qu___n   sh___p   b_____

1. s_ee___   3. gr_____n   5. sh_____

2. h_____   4. b_____   6. p_____p

Fill in the missing words.

> she   sheep   shop   queen
>
> see   he   green   bee

1. The _____ has three white _____.

2. _____ keeps the sheep in a pen.

3. The queen got them at a _____.

4. Jim saw a _____ leaf.

5. A big _____ sat on a red bud.

6. Did _____ _____ the bee?

My Spelling Dictation

Write the sentences.
Circle the spelling words.

1. _____

_____

2. _____

_____

Word Study

Read the words. Listen for the vowel sounds.
Write each word in the correct box.

kind	gave	most	cake
do	to	so	find
save	go	mine	blue

sound of **o** in **no**	sound of **i** in **time**	sound of **a** in **cave**	sound of **o** in **too**
_____	_____	_____	_____
_____	_____	_____	_____
_____	_____	_____	_____
_____	_____	_____	_____

Fill in the blank to complete each **-ind** word.

1. I need to ____ind my watch.

2. You must ____ind the key.

3. What ____ind of bee is it?

4. He is a ____ind person.

Spelling List

This Week's Focus:
- Review long and short vowel words
- Spell words with the consonant digraph **th**
- Recognize the short **u** sound in **was** and **of**
- Recognize the vowel sound in **a**

STEP 1 Read and Spell   **STEP 2 Copy and Spell**   **STEP 3 Cover and Spell**

fold

1. the

2. that

3. them

4. day

5. may

6. made

7. was

8. of

9. if

10. a

11. _____
   bonus word

12. _____
   bonus word

Fill in the boxes.

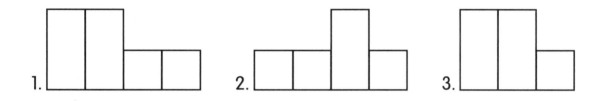

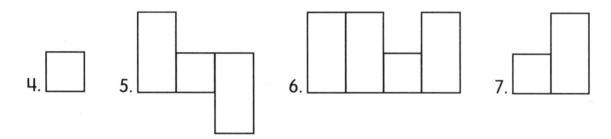

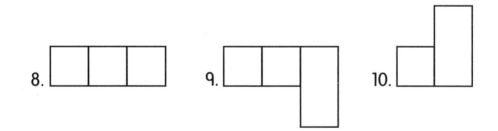

Find the Correct Word

Circle the word that is spelled correctly.

1. taht   that   4. wus   was

2. may   mai   5. dae   day

3. the   thu   6. them   thm

Word Meaning

Fill in the missing words.

day	of	them	if	a
that	was	made	the	may

1. Sunday is the first _____ of the week.

2. May I have _____ slice of cake?

3. Ask if you _____ come to my house.

4. Grandmother _____ a cake for _____.

5. Will _____ boys win the game?

6. What is in _____ big box?

7. Bob will come with us _____ he has time.

8. The little boy's balloon _____ red.

My Spelling Dictation

Write the sentences.
Circle the spelling words.

1. _____

_____

2. _____

_____

Word Study

Read the words. Listen for the sounds of **a**.
Write each word in the correct box.

may	sat	sand	made	game	flat
pan	cake	play	that	plant	stay

short **a** sound	long **a** sound
_____ _____	_____ _____
_____ _____	_____ _____
_____ _____	_____ _____
_____ _____	_____ _____

Say the word aloud. Circle the letters that stand for the first sound you hear.

the   them   that

Use these words to fill in the blanks.

the   them   that

1. May I go with _____?

2. _____ is a big dog!

3. I am not in _____ house.

Spelling List

This Week's Focus:
- Review short **u**, long **u**, and long **o** words
- Recognize the short **u** sound in **some** and **come**
- Add the ending **-ing** after doubling the final consonant

STEP 1 Read and Spell	STEP 2 Copy and Spell	STEP 3 Cover and Spell

fold

1. some

2. come

3. home

4. fun

5. funny

6. run

7. running

8. ran

9. us

10. use

11. _____
     bonus word

12. _____
     bonus word

Fill in the boxes.

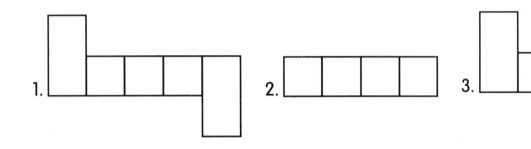

some   come   home   fun   funny

ran   run   use   us   running

1.

2.

3.

4.

5.

6.

7.

8.

9.

10.

Making New Words

Write the last letter a second time.
Then add **ing** to the word.

1. run   _running_

2. hit   _____

3. hum   _____

4. tag   _____

5. cut   _____

6. tap   _____

7. rub   _____

8. sit   _____

Fill in the missing word.

| some | come | home | fun | funny |
| ran | run | use | us | running |

1. Can you go to the circus with _____?

2. I _____ to the circus tent.

3. Sid and Tina were _____, too.

4. Will the clowns _____ here?

5. The _____ clowns jumped up and down.

6. _____ clowns were in a little car.

7. We had _____ at the circus.

8. It is time to go _____.

My Spelling Dictation

Write the sentences.
Circle the spelling words.

1. _____

_____

2. _____

_____

Word Study

Read the words. Listen for the vowel sounds.
Write each word in the correct box.

some	home	stone	fun
come	bone	don't	jump
joke	run	us	boat

the sound of **u** in **up**	the sound of **o** in **no**
_____ _____	_____ _____
_____ _____	_____ _____
_____ _____	_____ _____
_____ _____	_____ _____

Fill in each blank with the correct word.

ran   run   running

1. I _____ to meet the train this morning.

2. I like to _____ on the grass.

3. He is _____ in a big race today.

Spelling List

This Week's Focus:
- Review long **a** and long **i** words
- Spell the vowel sounds in **help**, **here**, and **want**
- Add the ending **-ing** after dropping the silent **e**
- Recognize homophones

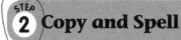

STEP **1** Read and Spell

STEP **2** Copy and Spell

STEP **3** Cover and Spell

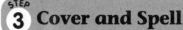

fold →

1. place

2. make

3. making

4. help

5. here

6. want

7. nice

8. to

9. two

10. into

11. _____
    bonus word

12. _____
    bonus word

Fill in the boxes.

> place   make   help   here   want
> nice   to   two   into   making

1. 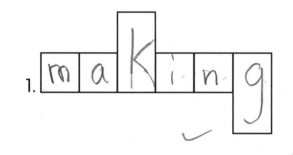 m a k i n g

2.  h e l p

3.  w a n t

4. 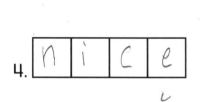 n i c e

5.  m a k e

6.  i n t o

7. t o

8. 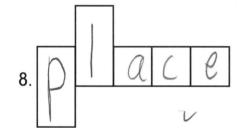 p l a c e

9.  h e r e

10. 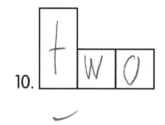 t w o

Find the Mistakes

Mark an **X** on the misspelled words.

1. ~~hep~~   help
2. make   ~~mak~~
3. ~~intwo~~   into
4. ~~nize~~   nice
5. place   ~~plaic~~

6. ~~makking~~   making
7. ~~twe~~   two
8. here   ~~heer~~
9. ~~wunt~~   want
10. to   ~~tou~~

Word Meaning

Write the missing words on the lines.

1. Can you __help__ me __make__ a cake?
   here, (help)   making, (make)

2. That is a __nice__ pet hamster.
   (nice), into

3. I __want__ __make__ cookies.
   (want), to   two, (make)

4. Let's go __to__ the mall.
   two, (to)

5. Toss the ball __into__ the hoop.
   (into), two

6. __Here__ is the __place__ to get ice cream.
   Help, (Here)   (place), make

My Spelling Dictation

Write the sentences.
Circle the spelling words.

1. _____

_____

2. _____

_____

Word Study

Make a new word by adding **ing**.
Be sure to follow the rules.

> • Just add **ing**
>
> play + ing = playing
>
> • Drop silent **e** and then add **ing**
>
> make + ing = making

1. bake ___baking___

2. want ___wanting___

3. sing ___singing___

4. ride ___riding___

5. take ___taking___

6. start ___Starting___

7. wash ___washing___

8. come ___coming___

9. chase ___chasing___

10. smile ___smiling___

Fill in the missing word.

1. Mom is ___baking___ cookies today.
   bake, (baking)

2. I will ___place___ the glass on the table.
   (place), placing

3. You are ___making___ a pretty picture.
   make, (making)

4. He must ___take___ the bus to work.
   (take), taking

Spelling List

This Week's Focus:
- Spell words with the final consonant blends **nd** and **st**
- Spell words with the final consonant digraph **th**
- Spell words with the /**k**/ sound spelled **ck**

STEP 1 Read and Spell	STEP 2 Copy and Spell	STEP 3 Cover and Spell

fold

1. send

2. pick

3. end

4. both

5. fast

6. last

7. must

8. just

9. bath

10. black

11. _____
    bonus word

12. _____
    bonus word

Visual Memory

Fill in the boxes.

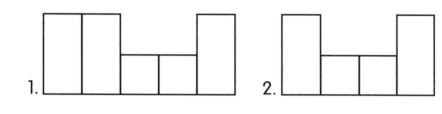

send   pick   end   both   fast
last   must   just   bath   black

1.

2.

3.

4.

5.

6.

7.

8.

9.

10.

Rhyming Words

Write the words that rhyme.

just   cast   trick   last   kick   past
send   sick   dust   mend   rust   bend

pick	**end**	**fast**	**must**
trick			

Fill in the missing words.

send	pick	end	both	fast
last	must	just	bath	black

1. The ballgame will _____ all day.

2. I was happy to _____ my prize.

3. Give _____ dogs a _____ in the tub.

4. His party will _____ at 5 o'clock.

5. The _____ car was so _____ it won the race.

6. Will Uncle Fred _____ me a letter?

My Spelling Dictation

Write the sentences.
Circle the spelling words.

1. _____

_____

2. _____

_____

Word Study

Add an ending to make a word. Write **th**, **st**, **ck**, or **nd**.

ba_____	sa_____	mo_____
chi_____	bla_____	ba_____

Fill in the missing letters.

1. Put the bla_____ chi_____ in the pen with the hen.

2. He mu_____ go home soon.

3. Did you take a ba_____?

4. I mu_____ run fa_____ or I will come in la_____.

Spelling List

This Week's Focus:
- Spell words with the long **i** or long **e** sound spelled **y**
- Review short and long vowel spelling patterns
- Study contractions

STEP 1 Read and Spell

STEP 2 Copy and Spell

STEP 3 Cover and Spell

fold

1. candy

2. went

3. sent

4. take

5. like

6. puppy

7. time

8. didn't

9. by

10. my

11. _____
   bonus word

12. _____
   bonus word

Fill in the boxes.

```
candy    went    sent    take    like
time    puppy    didn't    by    my
```

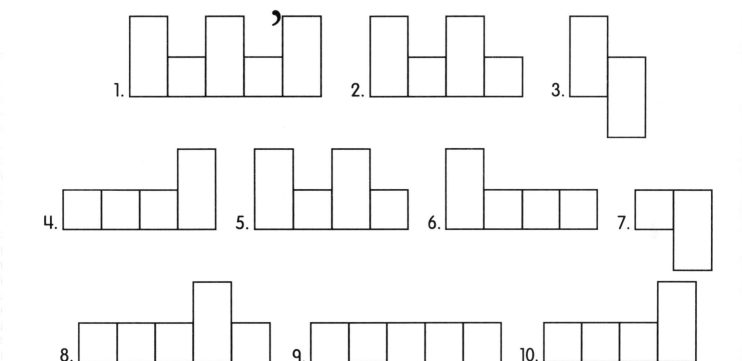

1.
2.
3.
4.
5.
6.
7.
8.
9.
10.

Contractions

Match the contractions to the correct words.

didn't - - - - - - - - is not

can't - - - - - - - - did not

isn't   cannot

I'm   it is

let's   I am

it's   let us

Word Meaning

Write the missing words on the lines.

1. It's _____ to feed the _____.
   time, like   sent, puppy

2. _____ mom _____ me to bed.
   By, My   sent, went

3. George _____ get to _____ a turn.
   like, didn't   take, time

4. I _____ cake and _____.
   take, like   candy, puppy

5. Jose _____ to sit _____ his dad.
   my, went   sent, by

6. I _____ my _____ on walks.
   didn't, take   by, puppy

My Spelling Dictation

Write the sentences.
Circle the spelling words.

1. _____

_____

2. _____

_____

Word Study

Read the words. Listen for the sounds of **y**.
Write each word in the correct box.

candy	by	your	funny
my	happy	yell	try
yam	yes	fly	puppy

sound of **y** in **sunny**	sound of **y** in **cry**	sound of **y** in **you**
_____	_____	_____
_____	_____	_____
_____	_____	_____
_____	_____	_____

Complete each rhyme with a spelling word.

1. Ask <u>Mandy</u>

   for some _____.

2. Where is the <u>tent</u>

   you were _____?

3. If you give me a <u>dime</u>

   I will tell you the _____.

4. Which racing <u>bike</u>

   do you really _____?

Spelling List

This Week's Focus:
- Practice spelling words with double consonants
- Distinguish between one- and two-syllable words

STEP 1 Read and Spell

STEP 2 Copy and Spell

STEP 3 Cover and Spell

fold

1. less

2. tell

3. well

4. will

5. still

6. off

7. letter

8. little

9. silly

10. happy

11. _____
   bonus word

12. _____
   bonus word

Fill in the boxes.

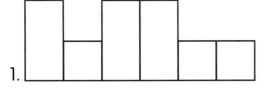

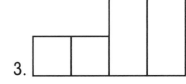
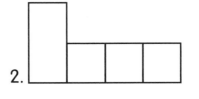

1.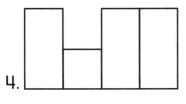

2.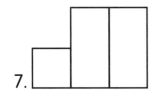

3.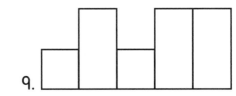

4.

5.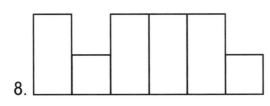

6.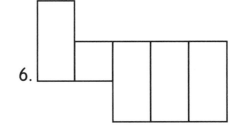

7.

8.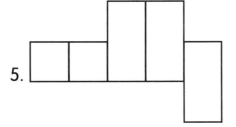

9.

10.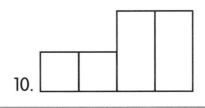

Find the Mistakes

Mark an **X** on the misspelled words.

1. wil	will		6. less	les
2. hapy	happy		7. litle	little
3. letter	leter		8. tel	tell
4. off	oof		9. well	wel
5. sily	silly		10. still	stell

Word Meaning

Write the missing words on the lines.

1. Mom was _____ to get a _____ from Grandma.
little, happy ; letter, less

2. Can you _____ me a _____ joke?
tell, will ; silly, well

3. I _____ take a _____ bit of candy.
well, will ; letter, little

4. It is _____ hot outside in the sun.
will, still

5. Turn _____ the TV when you go to bed.
little, off

6. Is six _____ than ten?
less, tell

My Spelling Dictation

Write the sentences.
Circle the spelling words.

1. _____

2. _____

Write the words that rhyme.

better	dress	four	seen
some	well	when	will

1. less _____

2. tell _____

3. still _____

4. letter _____

5. come _____

6. or _____

7. men _____

8. queen _____

Circle the number of syllables in each word.

1. letter   1   2

2. silly   1   2

3. well   1   2

4. less   1   2

5. little   1   2

6. happy   1   2

7. still   1   2

8. rabbit   1   2

9. bunny   1   2

10. black   1   2

11. into   1   2

12. two   1   2

13. lasted   1   2

14. place   1   2

15. help   1   2

16. making   1   2

Spelling List

This Week's Focus:
- Spell words in the **-oat**, **-ong**, and **-all** families
- Spell words with the vowel digraph **aw**

STEP 1 Read and Spell

STEP 2 Copy and Spell

STEP 3 Cover and Spell

fold

1. boat

2. coat

3. float

4. long

5. along

6. belong

7. paw

8. fawn

9. tall

10. wall

11. _____
bonus word

12. _____
bonus word

Fill in the boxes.

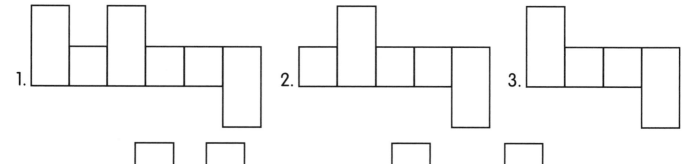

| boat | float | coat | long | along |
| belong | paw | fawn | tall | wall |

1.

2.

3.

4.

5.

6.

7.

8.

9.

10.

Spell Vowel Sounds

Add the missing letters. Write **aw**, **all**, or **oa**.

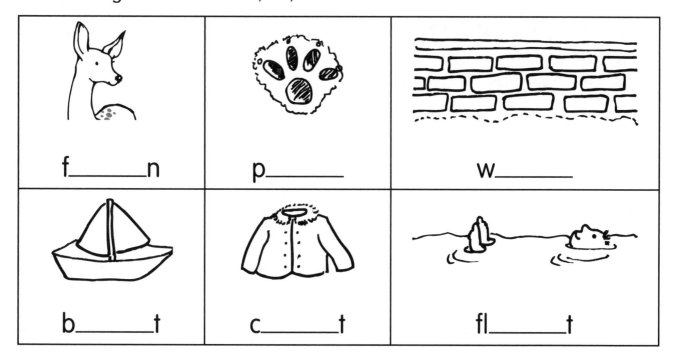

f_____n

p_____

w_____

b_____t

c_____t

fl_____t

Word Meaning

Write the missing words on the lines.

1. Can Allen _____ his _____ in the pond?
   float, fawn   coat, boat

2. Did the _____ _____ _____ to that man?
   long, wall   coat, float   along, belong

3. A _____ ran _____ the _____ _____.
   long, fawn   along, paw   boat, tall   wall, belong

4. The _____ dog has a large _____.
   coat, tall   paw, long

5. We took a _____ trip on a small _____.
   long, float   boat, fawn

6. The stone _____ runs _____ the road.
   boat, wall   belong, along

My Spelling Dictation

Write the sentences.
Circle the spelling words.

1. _____

_____

2. _____

_____

74

Word Study

Read the words. Listen for rhyming words.
Write each word in the correct box.

| boat | tall | coat | call | float |
| along | long | belong | wall | |

-all	-ong	-oat
call		

Complete each rhyme with a spelling word.

1. We will <u>float</u>

   in the _____.

2. At <u>dawn</u>

   we saw a _____.

3. The ball will <u>fall</u>

   from the tall _____.

4. We think we <u>belong</u>

   where the river is _____.

Building Spelling Skills

Spelling List

This Week's Focus:
- Spell words with the vowel digraphs **ai** and **ay**
- Review long **a** words with silent **e**

STEP 1 Read and Spell

STEP 2 Copy and Spell

STEP 3 Cover and Spell

fold

1. way

2. away

3. today

4. chain

5. wait

6. chase

7. play

8. played

9. rain

10. paint

11. _____
bonus word

12. _____
bonus word

Fill in the boxes.

| way | away | today | play | played |
| chain | chase | paint | wait | rain |

1.

2.

3.

4.

5.

6.

7.

8.

9.

10.

Spell Vowel Sounds

What is missing? Write **ai** or **ay**.

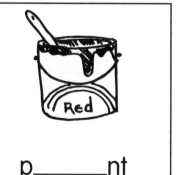

ch_____n

r_____n

p_____nt

w_____

w_____t

pl_____

tod_____

Word Meaning

Fill in the missing words.

way	away	today	play	played
chain	chase	paint	wait	rain

1. We like to _____ kickball.

2. Don't run _____!

3. Did Arnold's dog _____ the cat?

4. We are going to _____ the gate _____.

5. Carlos got wet in the _____.

6. Lock up your bike with that _____.

My Spelling Dictation

Write the sentences.
Circle the spelling words.

1. _____

_____

2. _____

_____

Word Study

Read the words. Listen for rhyming words.
Write each word in the correct box.

chain	way	chase	rain	play
case	face	away	today	pain
lane	race	main	stay	place

say	gain	vase
way		

Write a rhyming spelling word.

1. bay _____

2. bait _____

3. stayed _____

4. faint _____

5. vase _____

6. rain _____

Building Spelling Skills

Spelling List

This Week's Focus:
- Spell words with the vowel digraph **oo**
- Recognize the two sounds of **oo**
- Spell words with the initial consonant digraph **wh**

STEP 1 Read and Spell

STEP 2 Copy and Spell

STEP 3 Cover and Spell

fold

1. too

2. good

3. book

4. shook

5. school

6. when

7. what

8. took

9. who

10. soon

11. _____
   bonus word

12. _____
   bonus word

Fill in the boxes.

| too | good | book | shook | school |
| soon | what | when | who | took |

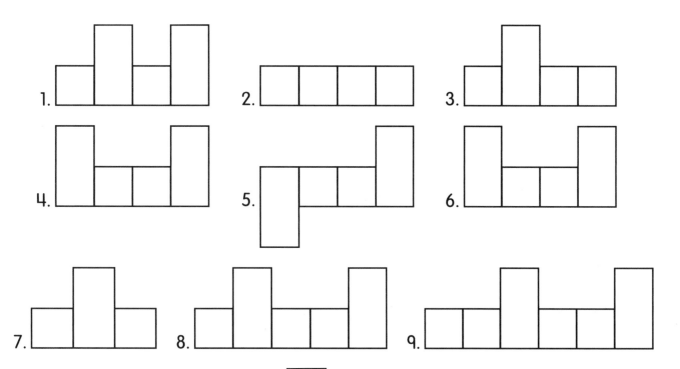

1.

2.

3.

4.

5.

6.

7.

8.

9.

10.

Find the Correct Word

Circle the words that are spelled correctly.

1. skool   school

2. good   gud

3. shook   shoock

4. whoo   who

5. took   twok

6. wat   what

7. when   wen

8. bock   book

Fill in the missing words.

| too | good | book | shook | school |
| soon | what | when | who | took |

1. It's time to go to _____.

2. Is that a _____ _____ to read?

3. He _____ the bell to make it ring.

4. _____ tore this book?

5. Can you tell me _____ is in the box?

6. Zeke wants to go swimming, _____.

My Spelling Dictation

Write the sentences.
Circle the spelling words.

1. _____

_____

2. _____

_____

Word Study

Read the words. Listen for the sounds of **oo**.
Write each word in the correct box.

school	good	cook	soon
shook	too	hook	took
boo	look	tool	who

sound of **oo** in **too**	sound of **oo** in **book**
boo _____ _____	_____ _____
_____ _____	_____ _____
_____ _____	_____ _____
_____ _____	_____ _____

Complete each rhyme with a spelling word.

1. The red <u>hood</u>

   looks very _____.

2. My teacher <u>took</u>

   the last _____.

3. The full <u>moon</u>

   will shine _____.

4. Will you <u>look</u>

   at what he _____?

Spelling List

This Week's Focus:
- Spell words with the vowel digraphs **ow** and **ou**
- Recognize the two sounds of **ow**

STEP 1 Read and Spell

STEP 2 Copy and Spell

STEP 3 Cover and Spell

fold

1. now
2. down
3. how
4. out
5. shout
6. about
7. our
8. house
9. slow
10. show
11. _____ bonus word
12. _____ bonus word

Fill in the boxes.

> now   down   how   out   shout
>
> about   our   house   slow   show

1.

2.

3.

4.

5.

6.

7.

8.

9.

10.

Spell Vowel Sounds

What is missing? Write **ow** or **ou**.

1. h _OU_ se

2. sh_____

3. d_____n

4. sh_____t

5. _____t

6. n_____

7. ab_____t

8. sl_____

9. h_____

10. _____r

11. sh_____

12. cl_____n

Fill in the missing words.

now	down	how	out	shout
about	our	house	slow	show

1. Don't _____ in the _____.

2. Can we go home _____?

3. _____ car is too _____.

4. The little boy jumped up and _____.

5. _____ will we get to the _____?

6. This book is _____ dinosaurs.

My Spelling Dictation

Write the sentences.
Circle the spelling words.

1. _____

   _____

2. _____

   _____

Word Study

Read the words. Listen for the vowel sounds.
Write each word in the correct box.

show	now	row	out	grow
our	go	down	how	shout
mow	about	bone	slow	house

sound of **ow** in **cow**	sound of **o** in **no**
_____ _____	_____ _____
_____ _____	_____ _____
_____ _____	_____ _____
_____ _____	_____ _____

Write a rhyming spelling word.

1. cow _____

2. shout _____

3. mouse _____

4. town _____

5. sour _____

6. show _____

Spelling List

This Week's Focus:
- Spell words with r-controlled vowels spelled **er**, **ir**, **ur**, and **ar**

STEP 1 Read and Spell	STEP 2 Copy and Spell	STEP 3 Cover and Spell

fold

1. her

2. girl

3. turn

4. hurt

5. first

6. were

7. card

8. part

9. start

10. are

11. _____
    bonus word

12. _____
    bonus word

Visual Memory

Fill in the boxes.

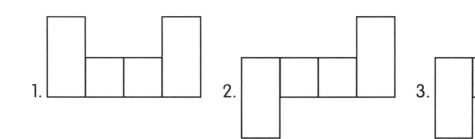

| her | girl | turn | hurt | first |
| were | card | part | start | are |

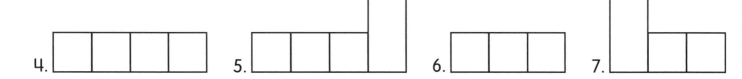

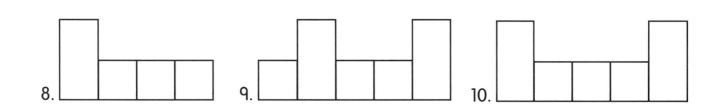

Find the Mistakes

Mark an **X** on the misspelled words.

1. That gril hurt her leg.

2. Did the game stard?

3. The ferst joke was funny.

4. It is Bob's tirn next.

Write the missing words on the lines.

1. She was the _____ _____ to play ball.
   her, first   hurt, girl

2. Margo _____ _____ hand when she fell.
   part, hurt   were, her

3. The girls _____ _____ of the team.
   are, turn   start, part

4. _____ the game with that _____.
   Are, Start   card, start

5. The next _____ is Kelly's.
   turn, were

6. Where _____ you yesterday?
   hurt, were

My Spelling Dictation

Write the sentences.
Circle the spelling words.

1. _____

   _____

2. _____

   _____

Word Study

Write the letters that spell the /**er**/ sound in the words.

> er   ir   ur

1. h_____

2. t_____n

3. g_____l

4. h_____t

5. w_____e

6. f_____st

7. st_____

8. c_____l

9. t_____key

10. n_____se

Find the Correct Word

Circle the words that are spelled correctly.

1. ar   are

2. card   kard

3. strat   start

4. part   pard

5. her   hur

6. gurl   girl

7. turn   tern

8. furs   first

9. wer   were

10. hurt   hert

Spelling List

This Week's Focus:
- Spell words with initial consonant blends **fl**, **bl**, and **st**
- Spell words in the **-ore**, **-ew**, and **-ing** families

STEP 1 Read and Spell

STEP 2 Copy and Spell

STEP 3 Cover and Spell

fold

1. more

2. store

3. stand

4. star

5. blew

6. flew

7. new

8. stone

9. sting

10. ring

11. _____
   bonus word

12. _____
   bonus word

Fill in the boxes.

> more   store   stand   star   blew
>
> new   flew   stone   sting   ring

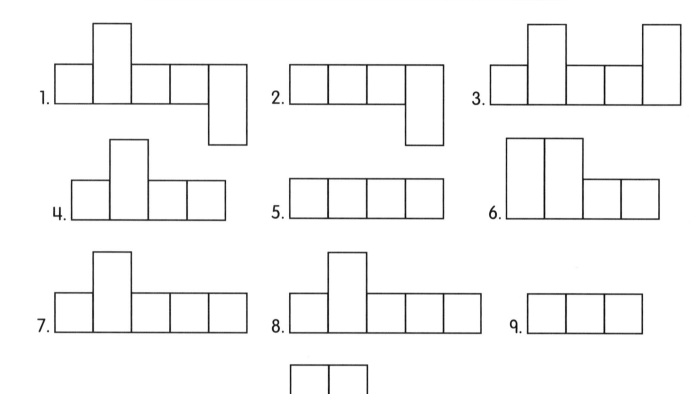

1.
2.
3.
4.
5.
6.
7.
8.
9.
10.

Find the Mistakes

Circle the misspelled words.

1. I went to the stor for Mom.

2. He blue up a red balloon.

3. The bird flu into a tree.

4. Did a bee styng Jamal?

5. Can I have some moor cookies?

Fill in the missing words.

more	store	stand	star	blew
new	flew	stone	sting	ring

1. There is a yellow _____ on Pam's hat.

2. She got a gold _____ at the _____.

3. The blue jay _____ back to her nest.

4. Did that bee _____ you?

5. We had to _____ in line to get on the bus.

6. Herman _____ out the candles on his cake.

My Spelling Dictation

Write the sentences.
Circle the spelling words.

1. _____

_____

2. _____

_____

Word Study

Add the missing letters. Write **st**, **bl**, or **fl**.

| _____ar | _____ocks | _____y |
| _____ackbird | _____ick | _____ag |

Circle the letters that make the same /**oo**/ sound as in **too**.

flew	moon	school	tool
you	who	too	do
to	chew	tooth	new

Complete each rhyme with a spelling word.

1. Are there <u>more</u>

   at the _____?

2. The rich <u>king</u>

   has a _____.

Building Spelling Skills

Spelling List

This Week's Focus:
- Spell words ending in **ve**
- Spell words with the consonant blends **fr** and **ld**
- Spell words with the final consonant digraph **ch**
- Recognize the short **u** sound spelled **ove**

STEP 1 Read and Spell

STEP 2 Copy and Spell

STEP 3 Cover and Spell

fold

1. have

2. give

3. love

4. from

5. live

6. friend

7. much

8. such

9. old

10. told

11. _____
    bonus word

12. _____
    bonus word

Fill in the boxes.

| have | give | love | from | live |
| friend | much | such | old | told |

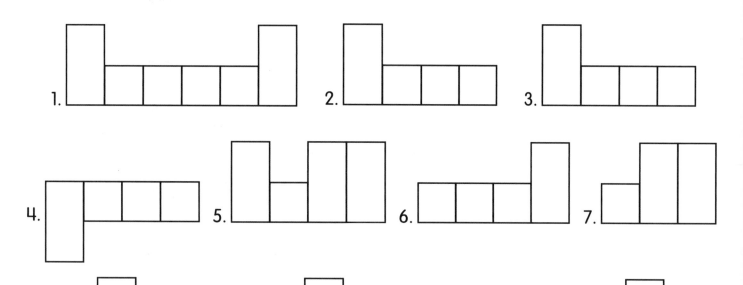

1.
2.
3.
4.
5.
6.
7.
8.
9.
10.

Rhyming Words

Match the words that rhyme.

give   such

old   live

much   glove

love   told

from   lend

friend   some

long   note

coat   some

too   song

rope   bunny

come   to

funny   soap

Write the missing words on the lines.

1. She got a letter _____ her best _____.
   from, give   told, friend

2. How _____ do you _____ your mother?
   such, much   live, love

3. Did Mark _____ in that _____ house?
   live, give   have, old

4. Will you _____ Donald part of your muffin?
   have, give

5. Alex _____ me to call him after school.
   from, told

6. You _____ _____ a cute dog!
   have, told   much, such

My Spelling Dictation

Write the sentences.
Circle the spelling words.

1. _____

   _____

2. _____

   _____

Word Study

Read the words. Listen for the vowel sounds.
Write each word in the correct box.

stove	have	glove	gave
give	shove	five	wave
love	dive	save	above

long vowel sound	short vowel sound
_____ _____	_____ _____
_____ _____	_____ _____
_____ _____	_____ _____

Write a rhyming spelling word.

1. live

_____

3. some

_____

5. bold

_____

2. dove

_____

4. such

_____

Use words from above to complete the sentence.

I _____ to _____ my friends presents.

Spelling List

This Week's Focus:
- Spell words with the initial /**y**/ sound
- Review long **i** words with the silent **e**
- Spell words with the initial consonant blend **dr**
- Spell words with the vowel digraph **aw**

STEP 1 Read and Spell

STEP 2 Copy and Spell

STEP 3 Cover and Spell

fold

1. you

2. your

3. yes

4. yell

5. drop

6. line

7. side

8. dress

9. draw

10. saw

11. _____ bonus word

12. _____ bonus word

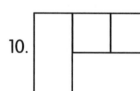
Fill in the boxes.

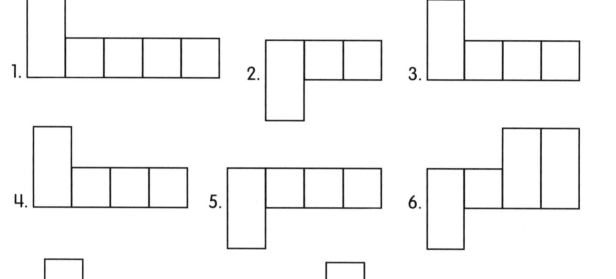

you   yes   yell   drop   line

side   your   dress   draw   saw

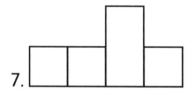

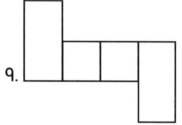

1.

2.

3.

4.

5.

6.

7.

8.

9.

10.

Find the Correct Word

Circle the word that is spelled correctly.

1. uoo   yeew   you

2. dess   dress   dreds

3. side   syde   sihd

4. zaw   saw   sah

5. grop   jrop   drop

6. line   yine   lin

Word Meaning

Fill in the missing word.

you	yes	yell	drop	line
side	your	dress	draw	saw

1. _____, you may go to the party.

2. Mary wore her red _____.

3. Stand on that side of the _____.

4. Will you _____ a clown for me?

5. Use the _____ to cut that wood.

6. Don't _____ your glass of milk.

7. I will _____ if you hit me.

My Spelling Dictation

Write the sentences.
Circle the spelling words.

1. _____

_____

2. _____

_____

Look at the pictures.
Fill in the missing letters. Write **tr**, **dr**, or **cr**.

_____uck	_____ess	_____ab
_____ee	_____own	_____um
_____icket	_____agon	_____umpet

Read the sentences.
Fill in the missing letters. Write **tr**, **dr**, or **cr**.

1. The baby began to _____y.

2. Throw that junk in the _____ash can.

3. Don't _____ip water on the clean floor.

4. The farmer planted a new _____op of corn.

5. We rode the _____ain to New York.

Spelling List

This Week's Focus:
- Spell words with diphthongs **oi** and **oy**
- Spell words that end with -**ther** or -**ter**
- Distinguish between one-, two-, and three-syllable words

STEP 1 Read and Spell

STEP 2 Copy and Spell

STEP 3 Cover and Spell

fold

1. boy

2. toy

3. oil

4. soil

5. other

6. mother

7. sister

8. boil

9. brother

10. father

11. _____
   bonus word

12. _____
   bonus word

Visual Memory

Fill in the boxes.

> boy   toy   oil   soil   boil
>
> mother   father   sister   brother   other

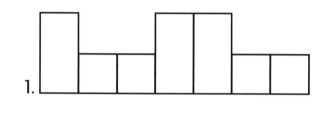
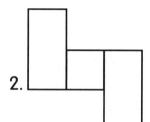
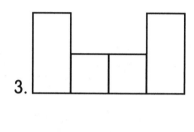

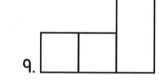

1.
2.
3.
4.
5.
6.
7.
8.
9.
10.

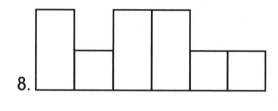

Word Study

What is missing? Write **oy** or **oi**.

1. b_____

2. b_____l

3. c_____n

4. R_____

5. s_____l

6. _____l

7. t_____

8. n_____se

Fill in the missing words.

> | | | | | |
> |---|---|---|---|---|
> | boy | toy | oil | soil | boil |
> | mother | father | sister | brother | other |

1. _____ and _____ went to town.

2. Angela is my baby _____.

3. Is that _____ your big _____?

4. The water will _____ when it gets very hot.

5. Jack likes this show, but I like the _____ one.

6. Plant seeds in the _____ in that pot.

My Spelling Dictation

Write the sentences.
Circle the spelling words.

1. _____

_____

2. _____

_____

Word Study

Change letters to make new words.

b   m   s   t   br

1. Roy   ____oy   ____oy

2. oil   ____oil   ____oil

3. other   ____other   ____other

4. twister   ____ister   ____ister

Circle the number of syllables in each word.

1. boy	1 2 3			5. mother	1 2 3
2. brother	1 2 3			6. family	1 2 3
3. sister	1 2 3			7. father	1 2 3
4. another	1 2 3			8. other	1 2 3

Complete each rhyme with a spelling word.

1. Don't put <u>oil</u>

   on the _____.

2. Ask the <u>boy</u>

   for a _____.

Spelling List

This Week's Focus:
- Spell words with final consonant digraphs **th** and **sh**
- Spell words with final consonant blends **ng** and **nk**

STEP 1 Read and Spell **STEP 2 Copy and Spell** **STEP 3 Cover and Spell**

fold

1. this

2. then

3. thing

4. thank

5. bank

6. with

7. wish

8. think

9. sing

10. these

11. _____
    bonus word

12. _____
    bonus word

Fill in the boxes.

| this | then | these | thing | think |
| bank | with | thank | sing | wish |

1.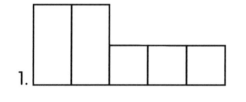

2.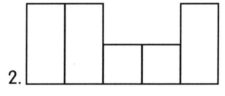

3.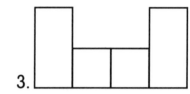

4.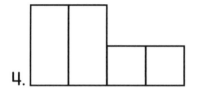

5.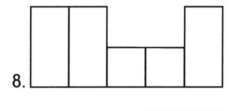

6.

7.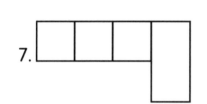

8.

9.

10.

Final Sounds

Add ending letters to make words.

| nk | ng | sh | th |

1. thi_____   thi_____

2. wi_____   wi_____

   wi_____   wi_____

3. si_____   si_____

4. ba_____   ba_____

   ba_____   ba_____

Fill in the missing word.

> this   then   these   thing   think
>
> bank   with   thank   sing   wish

1. I _____ I had a new bike.

2. What is this _____?

3. Katy put three dimes in her _____.

4. Did Lara say _____ you for the present?

5. Are _____ your socks?

6. Let's _____ a funny song.

7. Did you _____ the test was hard?

8. Put the chicks in _____ the mother hen.

My Spelling Dictation

Write the sentences.
Circle the spelling words.

1. _____

_____

2. _____

_____

Word Study

Write a rhyming spelling word.

1. blink _____   4. when _____

2. fish _____   5. miss _____

3. blank _____   6. ring _____

Listen for the /**th**/ and /**sh**/ sounds as you write the missing words on the lines.

1. _____ are good books.
   This, These

2. I got dressed and _____ went to school.
   then, this

3. You forgot one _____ on the test.
   think, thing

4. Did you say _____ you?
   thank, think

5. I _____ you could come for a visit.
   with, wish

6. May I go _____ you to the store?
   wish, with

7. Is _____ your kitten?
   these, this

111   Building Spelling Skills, Daily Practice • EMC 2706

Spelling List

This Week's Focus:
- Review words with the long **i** or long **e** sound spelled **y**
- Spell words with the long **e** sound spelled **ea**
- Spell words with initial blends **tr** and **fl**

STEP 1 Read and Spell

STEP 2 Copy and Spell

STEP 3 Cover and Spell

fold

1. why

2. try

3. trying

4. eat

5. mean

6. read

7. sunny

8. fly

9. treat

10. each

11. _____
    bonus word

12. _____
    bonus word

Visual Memory

Fill in the boxes.

why	try	trying	fly	eat
mean	each	read	treat	sunny

1.

2.

3.

4.

5.

6.

7.

8.

9.

10.

Beginning Sounds

Change letters to make new spelling words.

r m s fl tr cr wh

1. fry _____y

2. meat _____eat

3. funny _____unny

4. bean _____ean

5. bead _____ead

6. shy _____y

Write the answers.

1. Name a treat you can eat.

_____

2. Name three things that can fly.

_____ _____ _____

3. What can you do on a sunny day?

_____

4. Name two things you can read.

_____ _____

5. What happens if you are mean to an animal?

_____

6. Circle the word that asks a question.

    try   why   fly

My Spelling Dictation

Write the sentences.
Circle the spelling words.

1. _____

_____

2. _____

Word Study

Read the words. Listen for the vowel sounds.
Write each word in the correct box.

why	I	eat	see
time	treat	try	keep
mean	mine	read	pie
fly	each	bike	me

long **i**	long **e**
_____ _____	_____ _____
_____ _____	_____ _____
_____ _____	_____ _____
_____ _____	_____ _____

Complete each rhyme with a spelling word.

1. What may I <u>eat</u>

   as a small _____?

2. The baby bird will <u>try</u>

   his very best to _____.

3. The funny <u>bunny</u>

   likes when it is _____.

4. Will you <u>lead</u>

   when I _____?

     Building Spelling Skills, Daily Practice • EMC 2706

Spelling List

This Week's Focus:
- Spell words with initial consonant blends **tr** and **st**
- Add the ending **-ed** after doubling the final consonant
- Spell **say** and **said**
- Spell words with the short **u** sound

STEP 1 Read and Spell	STEP 2 Copy and Spell	STEP 3 Cover and Spell

fold

1. trip

2. tree

3. say

4. said

5. hop

6. train

7. number

8. stop

9. stopped

10. one

11. _____ bonus word

12. _____ bonus word

Fill in the boxes.

trip	say	tree	train	number
hop	said	stop	one	stopped

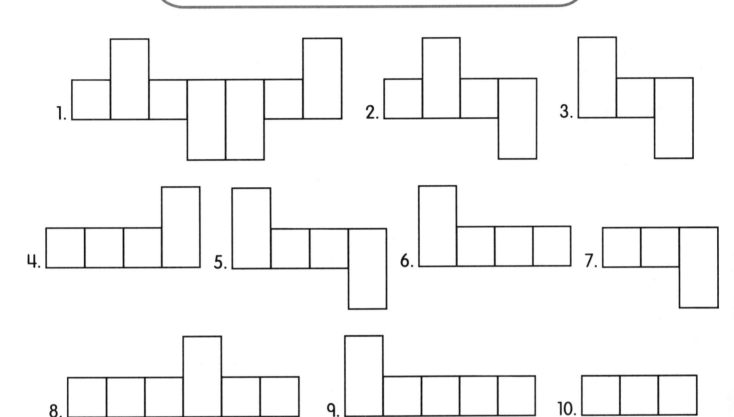

1.
2.
3.
4.
5.
6.
7.
8.
9.
10.

Rhyming Words

Match the words that rhyme.

say	skip
trip	play
one	hop
said	bed
number	fun
tree	rain
stop	lumber
train	we

Fill in the missing words.

| trip | say | tree | train | number |
| hop | said | stop | one | stopped |

1. Dad _____, "Let's go out for a pizza."

2. Maria rode a _____ to her grandmother's house.

3. I saw a bunny _____ to the carrots and then _____.

4. Martin was _____ _____ in the bike race.

5. They _____ by an apple _____ to rest in the shade.

6. What did the teacher _____ to her class?

My Spelling Dictation

Write the sentences.
Circle the spelling words.

1. _____

_____

2. _____

_____

Word Study

Double the last consonant and add **ed** to write a new word. When a word ends in a vowel and one consonant, double the last consonant and add **ed**.

1. trip _tripped_

2. stop _____

3. hop _____

4. pat _____

5. clap _____

6. hum _____

7. pin _____

8. plan _____

9. slip _____

10. chat _____

11. skip _____

12. drum _____

Complete the sentences using words you just made.

1. Ann _____ down the street.

2. He _____ on the ice.

3. Dad and I _____ a trip.

4. The man _____ his hands.

Spelling List

This Week's Focus:
- Spell words with a final **k** or **ck**
- Review the two sounds of the vowel digraph **oo**

STEP 1 Read and Spell

fold

1. stick
2. trick
3. back
4. zoo
5. root
6. quick
7. look
8. looked
9. pack
10. cook
11. _____
    bonus word
12. _____
    bonus word

STEP 2 Copy and Spell

STEP 3 Cover and Spell

Fill in the boxes.

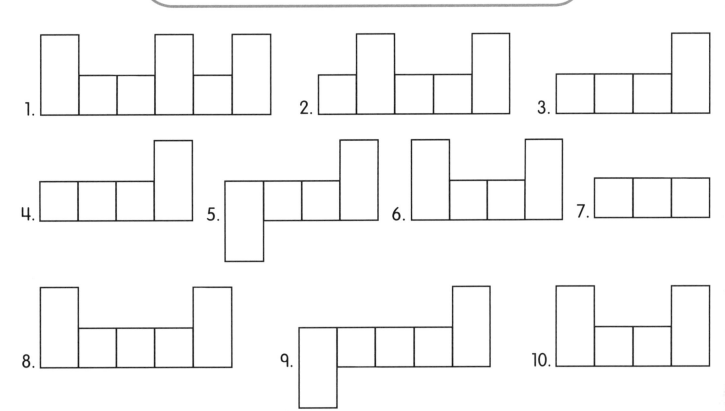

stick   trick   quick   back   zoo

root   look   cook   pack   looked

Rhyming Words

Match the words that rhyme.

stick	back	trick
look	quick	tack
pack	tool	cook
root	book	shoot
school	boot	pool

Write the missing words on the lines.

1. Roy _____ for his homework.
   look, looked

2. Mr. Green did a _____ with a big _____.
   trick, quick   zoo, stick

3. The chef will _____ dinner.
   look, cook

4. That weed had one long _____.
   cook, root

5. Put the _____ in the _____ of the car.
   pack, look   cook, back

6. Will you help me _____ for my book?
   look, cook

My Spelling Dictation

Write the sentences.
Circle the spelling words.

1. _____

   _____

2. _____

   _____

Listen for the vowel sounds.
Write **k** or **ck** on each line.
k becomes **ck** after one short vowel.

sti_____	clo_____	coo_____
du_____	boo_____	bri_____

loo_____   qui_____   ba_____

tri_____   pa_____   loo_____ed

Draw a line to match.

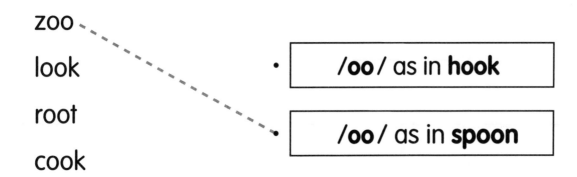

zoo

look

root

cook

/**oo**/ as in **hook**

/**oo**/ as in **spoon**

Spelling List

This Week's Focus:
- Spell words with the blends **pr**, **br**, and **ft**
- Spell two-syllable words
- Review long **a** words with silent **e**
- Spell words with the initial consonant digraph **ch**

STEP 1 Read and Spell

STEP 2 Copy and Spell

STEP 3 Cover and Spell

fold

1. birthday

2. people

3. present

4. candle

5. cake

6. children

7. gift

8. party

9. game

10. bring

11. _____
   bonus word

12. _____
   bonus word

Fill in the boxes.

people	present	candle	cake	children
birthday	party	game	bring	gift

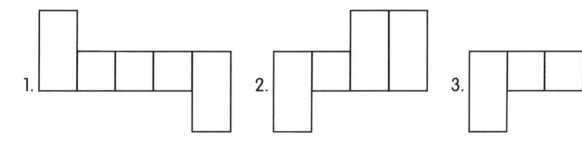

1.

2.

3.

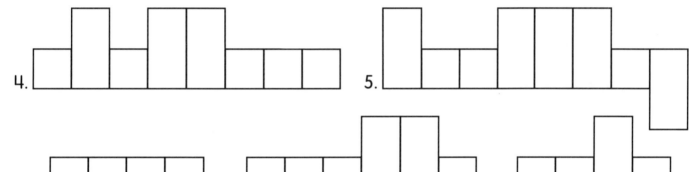

4.

5.

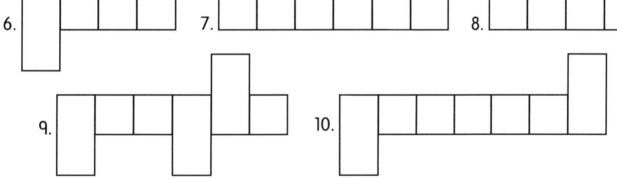

6.

7.

8.

9.

10.

Fill in the missing syllables to make spelling words.

1. _____dle

2. _____dren

3. pres_____

4. _____ty

5. _____day

6. peo_____

Word Meaning

Answer the questions.

1. Are children people?   Yes   No

2. Do **present** and **gift**
   mean the same thing?   Yes   No

3. Can you eat the candles
   on a birthday cake?   Yes   No

4. Will your mother let you play
   a card game in the house?   Yes   No

5. Do people bring presents
   to a birthday party?   Yes   No

6. Is your birthday the day
   your pet was born?   Yes   No

My Spelling Dictation

Write the sentences.
Circle the spelling words.

1. _____

   _____

2. _____

   _____

Write **pr** or **br** on each line.

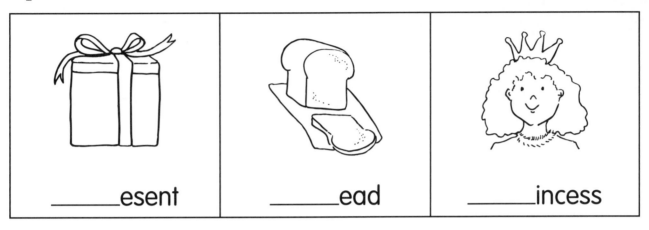

_____esent   _____ead   _____incess

_____etty   _____ize

_____ing   _____own

Look at the picture. Read the word aloud. Listen to the beginning sound.
Write the sound you hear at the beginning. Write **c** or **ch**.

_____ildren   _____an   _____ain

_____air   _____at   _____ake

Spelling List

This Week's Focus:
- Spell words with the vowel sound in **put** and **could**
- Spell words with the diphthongs **ou** and **ow**
- Recognize the short **u** sound in **something**

STEP 1 Read and Spell

STEP 2 Copy and Spell

STEP 3 Cover and Spell

fold

1. put

2. push

3. pull

4. could

5. would

6. found

7. round

8. around

9. something

10. brown

11. _____
   bonus word

12. _____
   bonus word

Fill in the boxes.

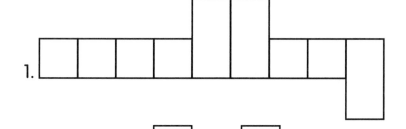

| put | round | pull | could | would |
| found | push | brown | around | something |

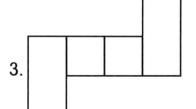
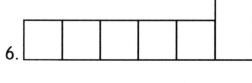
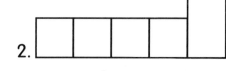
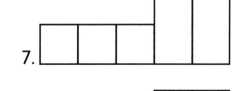
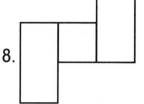

1.
2.
3.
4.
5.
6.
7.
8.
9.
10.

Spell Vowel Sounds

What is missing? Write **ou** or **ow**.

1. f_____nd

2. r_____nd

3. br_____n

4. cl_____n

5. ar_____nd

6. c_____

7. s_____nd

8. c_____nt

9. c_____ld

Fill in the missing words.

> | put | round | pull | could | would |
> |-----|-------|------|-------|-------|
> | found | push | brown | around | something |

1. Otis _____ his lost dog.

2. Betty hit the ball and ran _____ the bases.

3. She saw _____ funny on TV.

4. Will you help me _____ my sled up the hill?

5. That rock is _____ with _____ spots.

6. Burt said he _____ help paint the fence.

My Spelling Dictation

Write the sentences.
Circle the spelling words.

1. _____

_____

2. _____

_____

Word Study

Read the words. Listen for the vowel sounds.
Write each word in the correct box.

round	put	push	brown
could	hood	sound	pull
town	now	would	found

the sound of **ow** in **cow**	the sound of **oo** in **wood**
_____ _____	_____ _____
_____ _____	_____ _____
_____ _____	_____ _____
_____ _____	_____ _____

Write a rhyming spelling word.

1. bush

_____

2. would

_____

3. full

_____

4. crown

_____

5. hound

_____

6. sound

_____

Building Spelling Skills

Spelling List

This Week's Focus:
- Review long and short vowel sounds
- Listen for the initial consonant digraph **th**
- Spell two- and three-syllable words
- Recognize homophones (**no**, **know** and **to**, **two**)

STEP 1 Read and Spell	STEP 2 Copy and Spell	STEP 3 Cover and Spell

fold

1. they

2. their

3. many

4. any

5. anything

6. than

7. because

8. know

9. water

10. very

11. _____
   bonus word

12. _____
   bonus word

Fill in the boxes.

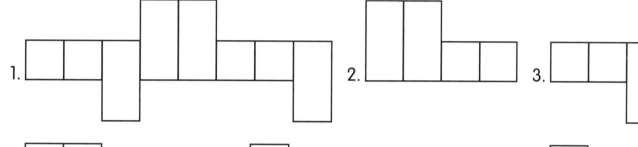

| they | their | many | because | than |
| know | water | very | any | anything |

1.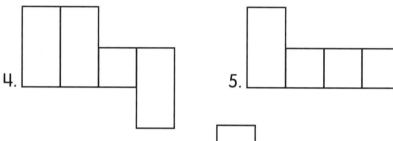

2.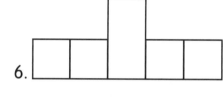

3.

4.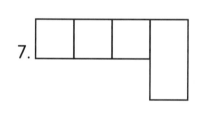

5.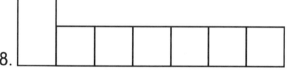

6.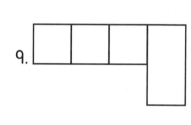

7.

8.

9.

10.

Find the Mistakes

Mark an **X** on the words that are misspelled.

1. enything   anything   5. water   wadder

2. because   becuz   6. miny   many

3. kno   know   7. verry   very

4. thay   they   8. any   iny

Word Meaning

Write the missing words on the lines.

1. Grandpa said, "You may have _____ you want."

    anything, any

2. Do you _____ how _____ fish there are?

    know, no   many, any

3. It is _____ hot _____ the sun is shining.

    very, any   because, know

4. Put _____ coats over _____ .

    their, there   their, there

5. When will _____ get here?

    they, them

6. Do you have _____ _____ to drink?

    any, anything   than, water

My Spelling Dictation

Write the sentences.
Circle the spelling words.

1. _____

    _____

2. _____

    _____

Word Study

Circle the sound made by the underlined letters.

1. th<u>ey</u>   a e i o
2. th<u>a</u>n   a e i o
3. an<u>y</u>   a e i o
4. kn<u>ow</u>   a e i o
5. n<u>i</u>ne   a e i o
6. ver<u>y</u>   a e i o
7. s<u>ee</u>   a e i o
8. c<u>oa</u>t   a e i o

9. pr<u>ey</u>   a e i o
10. s<u>o</u>   a e i o
11. man<u>y</u>   a e i o
12. m<u>y</u>   a e i o
13. pl<u>ay</u>   a e i o
14. p<u>ie</u>   a e i o
15. b<u>o</u>ne   a e i o
16. m<u>ea</u>t   a e i o

Homophones

Homophones are words that sound the same but are spelled differently.
Write the correct homophone on each line.

1. Do you _____ how to swim?
no, know

_____, you can't go swimming now.
No, Know

2. I have _____ goldfish in my tank.
to, two

Can we go _____ the zoo next Saturday?
to, two

Spelling List

This Week's Focus:
- Spell words with initial consonant digraphs **wh** and **th**
- Recognize and spell antonyms
- Spell compound words
- Recognize the short **e** sound in **again**

STEP 1 Read and Spell	STEP 2 Copy and Spell	STEP 3 Cover and Spell

fold

1. which

2. where

3. there

4. before

5. after

6. over

7. again

8. inside

9. outside

10. under

11. _____
   bonus word

12. _____
   bonus word

Fill in the boxes.

> | which | over | where | before | after |
> |-------|------|-------|--------|-------|
> | there | under | again | inside | outside |

1.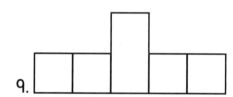

2.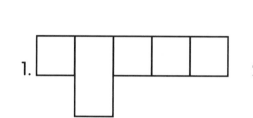

3.

4.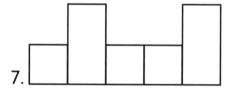

5.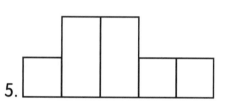

6.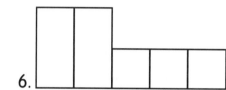

7.

8.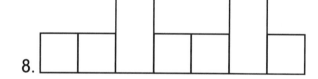

9.

10.

Opposites

Write the spelling word that means the opposite.

1. under _____

2. before _____

3. outside _____

4. here _____

Look at each picture. Circle the answer to the question.

Is the cat hiding
under the bed?

Yes
No

Is the clown before
the elephant?

Yes
No

Is the cover over
the birdcage?

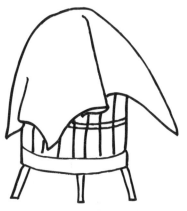

Yes
No

Has the dog gone inside
its doghouse?

Yes
No

Will you wear your raincoat
when you go outside?

Yes
No

Will you need a bath after
digging in the garden?

Yes
No

A compound word is two words put together to make a new word.
Make compound words here.

1. out + side   _____

2. in + to   _____

3. be + side   _____

4. no + thing   _____

5. birth + day   _____

Write the missing words on the lines.

1. _____ place would you like to visit_____?
   Which, Where   before, again

2. _____ will you go _____ school?
   There, Where   after, over

3. We will go _____ _____ it rains.
   over, outside   before, inside

4. _____ are two frogs _____ the tree.
   There, Over   before, under

5. We walk _____ the bridge to go _____
   over, again   inside, there

the fort.

Note: Use this form to track students' spelling progress.

Spelling Record Sheet

Building Spelling Skills

Students' Names															
1															
2															
3															
4															
5															
6															
7															
8															
9															
10															
11															
12															
13															
14															
15															
16															
17															
18															
19															
20															
21															
22															
23															
24															
25															
26															
27															
28															
29															
30															

Note: Reproduce this form twice for each student to track his or her progress.

My Spelling Record

Spelling List	Date	Number Correct	Words Missed

Spelling Test

Listen to the words.
Write each word on a line.

1. _____

2. _____

3. _____

4. _____

5. _____

6. _____

7. _____

8. _____

9. _____

10. _____

11. _____

12. _____

Listen to the sentences.
Write them on the lines.

1. _____

_____

2. _____

_____

Building Spelling Skills

Spelling List
Note: Reproduce this form to make your own spelling list.

STEP 1 Read and Spell	STEP 2 Copy and Spell	STEP 3 Cover and Spell

fold

1. _____ _____ _____
2. _____ _____ _____
3. _____ _____ _____
4. _____ _____ _____
5. _____ _____ _____
6. _____ _____ _____
7. _____ _____ _____
8. _____ _____ _____
9. _____ _____ _____
10. _____ _____ _____
11. _____ _____ _____
12. _____ _____ _____

Note: Reproduce this form to make your own word search or crossword puzzles.

Word Box

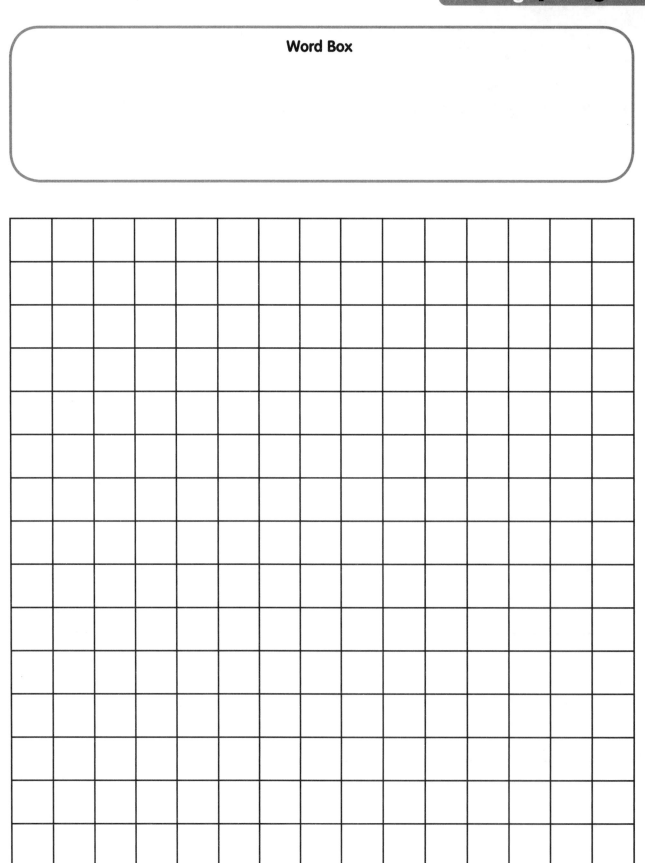

Building Spelling Skills

Dear Parents,

Attached is your child's spelling list for this week. Encourage him or her to practice the words in one or more of these ways:

1. Read and spell each word. Cover it up and write it. Uncover the word and check to see if it is correct.
2. Find the words on the spelling list in printed materials such as books and magazines.
3. Read a word aloud and ask your child to spell it (either aloud or written on paper).

Thank you for your support of our spelling program.

Sincerely,

Building Spelling Skills

Dear Parents,

Attached is your child's spelling list for this week. Encourage him or her to practice the words in one or more of these ways:

1. Read and spell each word. Cover it up and write it. Uncover the word and check to see if it is correct.
2. Find the words on the spelling list in printed materials such as books and magazines.
3. Read a word aloud and ask your child to spell it (either aloud or written on paper).

Thank you for your support of our spelling program.

Sincerely,

Student Spelling Dictionaries

Self-made spelling dictionaries provide students with a reference for words they frequently use in their writing.

Materials

- copy of "My Own Spelling Dictionary" form (page 147)
- 26 sheets of lined paper—6" x 9" (15 x 23 cm)
- 2 sheets of construction paper or tagboard for cover—6" x 9" (15 x 23 cm)
- crayons or markers
- glue
- stapler
- masking tape

Steps to Follow

1 Color and cut out the cover sheet form. Glue it to the front cover of the dictionary.

2 Staple the lined paper inside the cover. Place masking tape over the staples.

3 Guide students (or ask parent volunteers) to write a letter of the alphabet on each page.

What to Include

1. When students ask for the correct spelling of a special word, have them write it in their dictionary.

2. Include special words being learned as part of science or social studies units.

3. Include words for special holidays.

4. Include the common words students continue to misspell on tests and in daily written work.

5. Add color and number words if these are not on charts posted in the classroom.

— My Own —
Spelling
Dictionary

Name _____

— My Own —
Spelling
Dictionary

Name _____

You are a SUPER SPELLER!

Super Speller

Name

Congratulations!!

a	brown	fly	if
about	but	for	in
add	by	found	inside
after	cake	four	into
again	call	fox	is
all	came	friend	it
along	can	from	jam
an	candle	fun	just
and	candy	funny	kind
any	card	game	kite
anything	chain	gave	know
are	chase	get	land
around	children	gift	last
as	coat	girl	less
ask	come	give	letter
at	cook	go	like
away	could	going	line
back	cute	good	little
bank	day	got	live
bath	did	green	long
be	didn't	had	look
because	do	hand	looked
bee	doing	happy	love
before	down	has	made
belong	draw	have	make
big	dress	he	making
birthday	drop	help	man
black	each	her	many
blew	eat	here	may
boat	egg	him	mean
boil	end	his	men
bone	fast	home	mine
book	father	hop	mix
both	fawn	house	more
box	find	hot	most
boy	first	how	mother
bring	flew	hurt	much
brother	float	I	must

my	quick	start	try
name	rain	stick	trying
nap	ran	still	turn
new	read	sting	two
nice	red	stone	under
no	ride	stop	up
not	ring	stopped	us
now	root	store	use
number	round	such	very
of	run	sunny	wait
off	running	take	wall
oil	said	tall	want
old	save	tell	was
on	saw	than	water
one	say	thank	way
or	school	that	we
other	see	the	well
our	send	their	went
out	sent	them	were
outside	she	then	what
over	sheep	there	when
pack	shook	these	where
paint	shop	they	which
part	shout	thing	who
party	show	think	why
paw	side	this	will
people	silly	time	wish
pet	sing	to	with
pick	sister	today	would
place	slow	told	yell
play	small	too	yes
played	so	took	you
present	soil	toy	your
pull	some	train	zoo
puppy	something	treat	
push	soon	tree	
put	stand	trick	
queen	star	trip	

Answer Key

Page 21 *(Page 5)*
1-3, 9—but, had, did, hot
4. get
5, 7—in or on
6, 8—red or not
10. at

1. The pan is hot.
2. A dog is in the bed.
3. Can I get a cat?
4. His hat is red.

Page 22 *(Page 6)*
1. red
2. on
3. get
4. Did
5. hot
6. had

Page 23 *(Page 7)*

a	e	i	o	u
at	get	in	on	but
had	red	did	not	cup
pan	men	sit	hot	up

1. hot or not
2. had
3. did
4. but
5. get
6. red

Page 25 *(Page 9)*
1. big
2. fox, box, or has
3. nap
4. egg
5. jam
6. mix
7. as
8. has, fox, or box
9. pet
10. box, fox, or has

fox	jam	box
egg	as	has
mix	nap	pet

Page 26 *(Page 10)*
1. fox, box
2. big, egg
3. jam
4. has, nap
5. mix
6. pet

Page 27 *(Page 11)*
1. box
2. mix
3. as
4. pet
5. big

1. box   4. big
2. as   5. mix
3. pet   6. jam

Page 29 *(Page 13)*
1. small
2. hand or land
3. and
4. all
5. his
6. can
7. is or an
8. land or hand
9. call
10. an or is

an	small	can
is	and	hand
call	his	all
land	call	land

Page 30 *(Page 14)*
1. small
2. hand
3. land
4. call
5. all
6. his

Page 31 *(Page 15)*

a in an	a in all
can	small
cat	fawn
and	call
has	want
land	saw
hand	ball

1. land
2. call
3. can
4. his

Page 33 *(Page 17)*
1. men or man
2. for or him
3. it
4. man or men
5. him or for
6. we or or
7. up
8. four
9. or or we
10. I

1. Tim has for dogs.
2. That min had a hat.
3. Can wee go with them?
4. Is the cake four me?
5. Did Nina see hem?

Page 34 *(Page 18)*
1. four
2. for
3. man
4. men
5. I
6. up

Page 35 *(Page 19)*

man	can	fan
hen	ten	pen
coat	boat	goat

1. for
2. four
3. for
4. four

Page 37 *(Page 21)*
1, 5, 7, 10—save, name, came, or mine
2, 4—cute or ride
3. ask
6. add
8. bone
9. kite

1. came   6. bone
2. ask   7. mine
3. kite   8. add
4. ride   9. save
5. cute   10. name

Page 38 *(Page 22)*
1. cute
2. Save, bone
3. kite, mine
4. ask, ride
5. name
6. add
7. came

Page 39 *(Page 23)*

long vowels	short vowels
came	add
ride	up
save	him
cute	men
bone	ask
name	can
mine	got
kite	hand

1. add   3. mine
2. name   4. bone

Page 41 *(Page 25)*
1. sheep   6. got
2. shop   7. he or be
3. be or he   8. queen
4. she   9. see
5. bee   10. green

queen   sheep   bee

1. see   4. be or bee
2. he   5. she
3. green   6. peep

Page 42 *(Page 26)*
1. queen, sheep
2. She or He
3. shop
4. green
5. bee
6. he or she, see

Page 43 *(Page 27)*

e in me	e in pet
be	get
see	hen
queen	mess
she	bell
sheep	red
bee	then

1. bee   3. sheep
2. queen   4. shop

Page 45 *(Page 29)*
1. doing
2. most
3. no or so
4. gave
5. going
6. do
7. go
8. kind or find
9. find or kind
10. so or no

no—so, Bo, go, do, or to
mind—find, kind, bind, or rind
cave—Dave, gave, pave, rave, save, or wave
post—host, most, or post

go—going   find—finding
do—doing   sleep—sleeping

Page 46 *(Page 30)*
1. doing
2. kind
3. going
4. gave
5. most
6. find
7. go

Page 47 *(Page 31)*

o in no	i in time	a in cave	o in too
most	kind	gave	do
so	find	cake	to
go	mine	save	blue

1. wind or find
2. find
3. kind
4. kind

Page 49 *(Page 33)*
1. them
2. made
3. the
4. a
5. day
6. that
7. if or of
8. was
9. may
10. of or if

1. that   4. was
2. may   5. day
3. the   6. them

Page 50 *(Page 34)*
1. day
2. a or that
3. may
4. made, them
5. the
6. that or the
7. if
8. was

Page 51 *(Page 35)*

short **a**		long **a**	
sand	pan	may	cake
plant	flat	stay	game
sat	that	made	play

(Th)e (Th)em (Th)at

1. them
2. That
3. the

Page 53 *(Page 37)*
1. funny
2. come or some
3. fun
4. some or come
5. run, use, or ran
6. use, run, or ran
7. us
8. running
9. home
10. ran, use, or run

1. running	5. cutting
2. hitting	6. tapping
3. humming	7. rubbing
4. tagging	8. sitting

Page 54 *(Page 38)*
1. us
2. ran
3. running
4. come
5. funny
6. Some
7. fun
8. home

Page 55 *(Page 39)*

u in **up**	**o** in **no**
some	home
fun	stone
come	bone
jump	don't
run	joke
us	boat

1. ran
2. run
3. running

Page 57 *(Page 41)*
1. making
2. help
3. want
4. nice
5. into or make
6. make or into
7. to
8. place
9. here
10. two

1. ~~help~~ help
2. make ~~mak~~
3. ~~two~~ into
4. ~~nice~~ nice
5. place ~~place~~
6. ~~makking~~ making
7. ~~two~~ two
8. here ~~here~~
9. ~~want~~ want
10. to ~~to~~

Page 58 *(Page 42)*
1. help, make
2. nice
3. want, two
4. to
5. into
6. Here, place

Page 59 *(Page 43)*

1. baking	6. starting
2. wanting	7. washing
3. singing	8. coming
4. riding	9. chasing
5. taking	10. smiling

1. baking
2. place
3. making
4. take

Page 61 *(Page 45)*
1. black
2. fast or last
3. bath or both
4. pick or just
5. must or send
6. last or fast
7. end
8. send or must
9. both or bath
10. just or pick

pick	**end**
trick	mend
sick	send
kick	bend

fast	**must**
cast	just
last	dust
past	rust

Page 62 *(Page 46)*
1. last
2. pick
3. both, bath
4. end
5. black, fast
6. send

Page 63 *(Page 47)*

ba<u>th</u>   sa<u>ck</u>   mo<u>th</u>
chi<u>ck</u>   bla<u>ck</u>   ba<u>nd</u>

1. black, chick
2. must
3. bath
4. mu<u>st</u>, fa<u>st</u>, la<u>st</u>

Page 65 *(Page 49)*
1. didn't
2. take or like
3. by
4. sent or went
5. like or take
6. time
7. my
8. candy
9. puppy
10. went or sent

© Evan-Moor Corp.   153   Building Spelling Skills, Daily Practice • EMC 2706

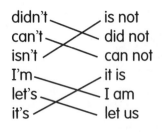

didn't — is not
can't — did not
isn't — can not
I'm — it is
let's — I am
it's — let us

Page 66 *(Page 50)*
1. time, puppy
2. My, sent
3. didn't, take
4. like, candy
5. went, by
6. take, puppy

Page 67 *(Page 51)*

y in **sunny**	y in **cry**	y in **you**
candy	by	your
funny	my	yell
happy	try	yam
puppy	fly	yes

1. candy
2. sent
3. time
4. like

Page 69 *(Page 53)*
1. letter
2. less
3. will or well
4. tell
5. silly
6. happy
7. off
8. little
9. still
10. well or will

1. ~~wil~~ will   6. less ~~les~~
2. ~~hapy~~ happy   7. ~~litle~~ little
3. letter ~~leter~~   8. ~~tel~~ tell
4. off ~~of~~   9. well ~~wel~~
5. ~~sily~~ silly   10. still ~~stil~~

Page 70 *(Page 54)*
1. happy, letter
2. tell, silly
3. will, little
4. still
5. off
6. less

Page 71 *(Page 55)*
1. dress   5. some
2. well   6. four
3. will   7. when
4. better   8. seen

1. 2   9. 2
2. 2   10. 1
3. 1   11. 2
4. 1   12. 1
5. 2   13. 2
6. 2   14. 1
7. 1   15. 1
8. 2   16. 2

Page 73 *(Page 57)*
1. belong
2. along
3. long
4. coat
5. fawn
6. boat
7. paw
8. float
9. tall
10. wall

f<u>aw</u>n   p<u>aw</u>   w<u>all</u>
b<u>oat</u>   c<u>oat</u>   fl<u>oat</u>

Page 74 *(Page 58)*
1. float, boat
2. long, coat, belong
3. fawn, along, tall, wall
4. tall, paw
5. long, boat
6. wall, along

Page 75 *(Page 59)*

-all	-ong	-oat
call	long	boat
tall	belong	float
wall	along	coat

1. boat
2. fawn
3. wall
4. long

Page 77 *(Page 61)*
1. today
2. paint
3. play
4. chase or chain
5. away
6. wait
7. way
8. played
9. chain or chase
10. rain

ch<u>ai</u>n   r<u>ai</u>n   p<u>ai</u>nt

way   wait   play   today

Page 78 *(Page 62)*
1. play
2. away
3. chase
4. paint or chain, today
5. rain
6. chain

Page 79 *(Page 63)*

say	**gain**	**vase**
way	chain	chase
play	rain	case
away	pain	face
today	lane	race
stay	main	place

1. way, away, today, or play
2. wait
3. played
4. paint
5. chase
6. chain